One Man and LEJOG

End-to-End on Two Wheels in Two Weeks

Antony Last

One Man and LEJOG
End-to-End on Two Wheels in Two Weeks

Maps: Contain Ordnance Survey data
© Crown copyright and database right 2010

Photos: Copyright © 2010 Antony Last

Text: Copyright © 2010 Antony Last
(originally published at http://onemanandlejog.wordpress.com)

British Library Cataloguing in Publication Data.
A cataloguing record for this book is available from the British Library

ISBN 978-1-4461-7196-7

To Kathryn

Contents

TONY
FLORA
40405
adidas

Flora London Marathon
Sunday 13th April 2008

Prologue: A Bit About Me

Before starting I'd just like to say however you've ended up with a copy of this book in your hands I hope it offers you a bit of an interesting read or perhaps a bit of advice if you yourself are planning on taking on the challenge that is a LEJOG.

A LEJOG (Lands End to John O'Groats) is probably the longest journey you can undertake in Britain. The straight-line distance between the two is approximately 600 miles, but that would involve passing through several stretches of the Irish Sea. The distance by land is roughly 900 miles although the route I chose to take topped 1,000 as I visited the most southerly and northerly points (Lizard Point and Dunnet Head respectively) along the way. Anyway, I digress. A bit about me...

So, yeah...I'm pretty much your standard twenty-eight year-old (at the time of writing!) Londoner I guess. I like my football, I like my beer and in the last couple of years I've decided that life's about more than simply earning more than the next person - it's what you make of it that counts.

I ran the London Marathon in 2008 and got round in just under five and a half hours. It's a time I'd like to beat but, having been rejected in the ballot for two years running, I thought it was time to set myself another challenge. I've always fancied the idea of a long-distance cycle tour and after researching various options in a bit more detail I thought a LEJOG was a suitable challenge to attempt.

A common question from people was 'why did you go from the bottom of Britain up to the top as opposed to the other way?'. Well, despite popular belief, it's statistically downhill going that way but that's not the only reason...

The terrain in Devon and Cornwall is actually more demanding than the Highlands with repetitive short, sharp climbs the norm rather than slow, undulating hills. Tackling that whilst fresh (ha!) sounded more appealing than knowing that it's only going to get harder at the end! Also, the winds in Spring and Summer are traditionally south-westerly so, in theory, there was more chance of a tailwind to help me on my journey.

I hastily set up a blog to pretty much commit myself to the journey, but doing so also gave me a tool to note down my thoughts and experiences before, during and after the event that I could look back on. It is those words that have now made their way onto the printed pages you're holding.

Collating the words I wrote alongside the photos I took along the way into a physical record of my journey is perhaps a little narcissistic but there's not going to be many occasions in my life whereby I record two weeks in quite as much detail so it's nice to commit it to physical print.

If I'm honest, the initial motivation was purely self-indulgent. I wanted to prove to myself that I could complete a challenge such as this and say 'I've done that'. I quickly realised, however, that undertaking such a task does offer an opportunity to help others and decided to direct anybody that wished to sponsor my effort to The Stroke Association. As I finalised this book, the total figure raised was just over £1,000 including Gift Aid. I'd like to thank everybody that sponsored me along the way. It really was and is appreciated by both myself and the charity.

Well, that's pretty much it. What follows is an account of my twelve-day cycle from Lands End to John O'Groats. If you do have any questions at all then please do get in touch with me at antony@apsleyway.co.uk and I'll do my best to answer them!

Thank you.

'It is by riding a bicycle that you learn the contours of a country best, since you have to sweat up the hills and coast down them. Thus you remember them as they actually are, while in a motor car only a high hill impresses you, and you have no such accurate remembrance of country you have driven through as you gain by riding a bicycle'

- Ernest Hemingway

Day One: Lands End to St. Agnes

or, The One Where Tony Realised He Wasn't in Kansas Any More...

'Oh dear God, not another hill...which bastard decided to route the roads like this...how on Earth am I going to get through the whole journey?!'. Yep, you've guessed it...that's me. Funny thing is it was on the short trip to get to the start in Lands End! More on this later...

There was a good start to my adventure as I somehow managed to miss the turn to Paddington and ended up meandering the streets of London trying to find the station - oh well, what's another mile and a half in the grand scheme of things?!

Got to the station and boarded the Riviera Express. Have to say, it's all very Poirot or James Bond with the narrow corridors and small cabins - I half expected to be awoken by a Soviet temptress informing me that 'the snow lies deep in Moscow'...

That didn't happen though. I settled into my berth, watched a bit of on-board telly and drifted off as the train pulled out and headed westwards.

To say it was a good night's sleep would be a lie, but I'm not sure it would have been much better had I done the preparation with a day train down and spent the night in Penzance or Lands End.

I was up by six o'clock and watched a bit more telly before the knock on my door let me know my breakfast was ready; bacon roll and a pot of tea, lovely!

We rolled into Penzance bang on time and the seaside town looked lovely bathed in the late-May sunshine. I couldn't have asked for a better start to the journey as I readied my bike, clipped myself in and set off...

I'd decided to head down to Lands End via the scenic back roads rather than the more direct A30. It was a lovely start, following the shore for a good spell, but I was questioning the decision as I hit the

...hmm, that hill training that people talked about was obviously for a reason! I struggled my way up this 'beast' of a hill, and continued my way up and down numerous climbs (the downhills quite exhilarating, the uphills less so!) before joining the A30 for the run-in to Lands End.

That last mile into Lands End was wonderful, a lovely downhill roll and I couldn't help but think how nice a finish it would be on a day like this, in the sunshine and with Penzance and the train home just twelve miles away. Oh well!

I sat for a bit as people packed up some flags from the finish line (found out later it was a John O'Groats to Lands End run, sixty miles a day for two months...!), reset my cycle computer and then pootled over to the start line. I asked one of the official runners' photographers to take a picture of me on the start line, had a bit of banter with them about the distance I had ahead and that was it...my journey had begun!

I travelled back towards Penzance on the A30 and the difference in the journey was amazing. Rolling hills, warm sunshine, a lovely view over the sea and a far better road surface made it a far more pleasurable journey than on the local roads.

It was about five miles to go 'til Penzance I realised I didn't have my RoadID bracelet on... must have left it on the train! As I was due to go past Penzance anyway, I made the decision to detour back in and see if I could retrieve it.

The staff at Penzance station were excellent. A phone call from the information desk saw me introduced to Kane, who directed me to the depot and met me there to see if he could find it on the train that was in the sidings. Well, he managed to find it and I got it back...thanks Kane, and good luck with your mammoth car journey later on!

It was here at the depot that I got chatting to someone and explained that I'd taken the, er, scenic route down to Lands End. His comments of 'really? Is that not a bit hilly?!' made me realise that perhaps it wasn't the best option for my first leg if even the locals consider it a challenge!

Fully equipped once again it was onto Lizard, and I made good time on the trip down south. Another random individual was persuaded to take a photo and I decided to have lunch in England's most southern cafe overlooking the seemingly endless sea.

After the break the trip back up towards St. Agnes was hard work. A headwind has developed and the road signs were seemingly only there to taunt me - Redruth was a waypoint and seeing 'Redruth 8', 'Redruth 8', 'Redruth 7' and then 'Redruth 8' as I travelled wasn't that appreciated!

After making it to Redruth I looked on the Garmin to see how many miles I had left to cover and my ETA into St. Agnes. It was a bit of a concern to see that it thought I had fifteen miles less than I made it and an ETA that would mean I had to cycle in at 20mph for the rest of the day... which wasn't going to happen!

It took me a while longer whilst cycling to remember that I'd reset my Cateye cycle computer back at Lands End, the GPS was right and it was a pleasant sight as the Penkerris Guest House rolled into view!

After settling in and showering I had a wander into St. Agnes' 'town centre' and a stroll down to the beach. It's a lovely little village and the fish and chips I had for tea were as good as seaside fish and chips should be!

Back to Penkerris and a bit of telly and an early night awaited. Day one, done...

Stats for Saturday 15th May 2010

Distance..66 miles
Time in saddle...5hrs 18mins
Average speed...12.5mph
Maximum speed..37.8mph

Day Two: St. Agnes to Westward Ho!

or, The One Where Tony Hits Forty

What. A. Day! I'd initially planned this trip thinking I'd be up and away from wherever I was staying early doors, and on the road by 07.30ish - giving me time to make as many stops as I felt necessary, yet still getting to my destination for the night with a bit of time to potter around before bed.

This plan was thrown into disarray at the earliest opportunity when it became apparent that breakfast was served from 08.30...bugger! So, after a later breakfast than planned I was out on the road at about 09.15. With this in mind, and ninety five miles to cover, I estimated I'd hit the Ho! at 19.00ish...I'd be happy with that. A quick check on the YHA website told me that the hostel's reception closed at 20.30 so I had a bit of leeway.

It was a much cooler day, with the sun hiding itself behind a solid cloud cover as I headed off resplendent in legwarmers and armwarmers... very 'Eighties', although arguably less tasteful!

From the start I was winding through Cornwall's minor roads. Whilst picturesque, the 'temporary road surface' signs were a clue that the roads weren't great to ride on. Any descent had to be taken cautiously; loose chippings littering every bend, almost inviting the front wheel in before throwing it out.

Seven miles of nervous cornering later I reached a crossroads and, after consulting the GPS, made the decision to scrap my initial route plan and simply hit the A-roads. Nowhere near as nice to look at, but a far, far better surface to cycle on with the minor roads giving me no confidence and therefore slowing me down.

So to the A30 I went, and It's fair to say It was a little busier than the lanes I'd just left! I settled myself into the hard shoulder and set on my way.

With the start to the day not quite going to plan

I'd re-assessed and mentally split the day ahead into three chunks. St. Agnes to Wadebridge, then to Bude and finally to Wesward Ho! Three thirty mile chunks, although each one containing a fairly big climb.

Whilst on the road, I also made the decision to give Padstow a swerve - not only was it a detour I didn't really feel like taking, it was also only on the plan for fish and chips at Rick Stein's restaurant. As I'd now get there about eleven o'clock, I thought it was too early to eat that heavy a meal.

I was making good headway, the main road offering some lovely sweeping descents and with the road surface much better I had confidence to let the bike do the work without feeling the need to brake.

Approaching Wadebridge I stopped off at some services for some food and drink. Anyone at the gym that might be reading) I had a lovely egg and nut feast; no rubbish. None at all...anyone else, I'm making my way cross country at the moment sustained between meals by Snickers, Coke and strawberry milk - it's quick, easy and is doing me alright so far!

I filled up my water bottles and snacked on Mars' fine blend of peanuts, nougat and chocolate. A drizzle started to fall, swiftly followed by a heavy shower. Someone was obviously looking down on me, as the skies cleared by the time I was ready to set off again...what luck!

Just past Wadebridge I turned onto the majestically titled Atlantic Highway (the A39), which I saw I could just sit on for the rest of my journey rather than meander around the back roads as initially planned. Not the most adventurous of routes, but with the distance involved in the day I didn't want to try my luck too much.

There was a lovely descent as the A39 started and with the road clear I settled in to enjoy it -

towards the bottom I knew it was a quick one, a glance at the Cateye once I was at a more sedate speed I confirmed it was...42.8mph, whoop!

The rest of the second leg wasn't quite as eventful and I'd go as far to say it was a bit of a slog to be honest. I was starting to doubt if I'd get to my finishing point in time. Dinner was had in the glamourous settings of St. Kew's service station forecourt - Costcutter's chicken and stuffing sandwich, whilst nice, probably doesn't compare with Mr. Stein's fare!

As I entered the second leg of the day roadies started appearing, heading in the opposite direction on some really nice bikes. Stopping off at the next garage, someone on the forecourt commented 'impromptu feed stop, hey?' which is when I realised it was an organised sportive event. I got chatting to a competitor that had stopped off for a cup of tea (funny how the mind works, hey?), and he'd opted to switch to the medium route which was 'only' seventy five miles. We bid each other well and set off in opposite directions.

I passed Bude in good spirits, the last fifteen miles or so having gone really well, and entered the final leg of the journey...and what a leg it was! From out of nowhere fog descended on top of me, literally descended with visibility down to about two hundred yards at best. To not have a clue what was coming up ahead was a little bit of a concern, with climbs made harder as the summits weren't visible and descents taken more warily. Then, to top it all off, the rain came...

...proper rain. Atlantic rain. Oh well, it had to come some time I guess! After about an hour or so (ten miles) it eased off, but it was 'fun' whilst it lasted. As it stopped I reached a layby with a picnic area. My saddlebag had started to swing a bit and whilst it wasn't holding me up at all I decided to stop off and have a look to see if I could stop it.

Well, for the second time of the day I felt that someone must have been looking down on me. As I took the bag off the rack, the attachment snapped. Sheared straight off. So much for British-made quality! Now, whilst this was probably quite funny to an outsider, I still had twenty miles to cover, and a bag that no longer attached to the bike. Oh dear.

Remember I said it was a picnic area? Well, I sat myself on the bench and had a think...bodge job it was! Cable ties and duct tape used and, whilst not perfect it looked like my handiwork would hold. Hurrah!

I carried on with thoughts running through my head wondering just how I was going to sort this issue out - there was still nine hundred miles or so to cover. This wasn't in the plan!

With about ten miles to go, just as I started to ascend a climb that I'd have preferred not to be there I heard a squealing from the back tire...my bodge had started to fail and the bag was sitting on the mudguard. I moved over to the verge and started to think about what to do...

In the end I opted to spend the last spell of the day with the bag balanced on my bars. Not the best way to travel and certainly not the safest. I have absolutely no idea how I hit my planned arrival time, but I gingerly rolled onto Westward Ho! at around 18.30!

After booking into the hostel I got changed out of my wet clothes and went for a wander to clear my head. A small portion of chips overlooking the sea (just to test them, of course!) and a chance to think about what to do with my stuff.

I know in a couple of days I go through Bristol, which will definitely have a shop that can help - but 'til then I need to get my kit around. A rucksack's not ideal for cycling with, but I packed light with just under four kilos of bits (more reason to be

pissed off with the broken rack...maximum weight of ten kilos my arse!) so it would probably get me through a couple of days. Now, where to get one...

Whilst the iPhone's capable of browsing the web, it can be pretty painful so I called my brother and got him in front of a computer. Turns out that there's an outlet village just three and a half miles out of Westward Ho!, and it's got two mountaineering stores...result!

Picked up some sandwiches that were on offer and an apple pie with custard for tea (I know how to live!) and headed back to the hostel for the evening.

Ah, the hostel...lovely place, but it does appear to be a haven for oddballs! There's four people booked in including myself; one lad who's walking the Devon coastline, a sixty seven year old gentleman who 'has to leave Leicester at least once a month or I go mad' and a boy who must be in his late teens that's been sent here for a week by his mother to 'sort himself out'. What a world!

So the plan tomorrow is to head out to Atlantic Village for nine o'clock opening time (so pleased it's not a Sunday), pick up a bag and then head back to the hostel to pick up my stuff and head on my way with hopefully a proper solution available in Bristol the next day. It's set a long day time-wise tomorrow, I'm glad it's a shorter one in distance...

Stats for Sunday 16th May 2010

Distance..82 miles
Time in saddle................................6hrs 5mins
Average speed.................................13.4mph
Maximum speed..............................42.8mph

Total distance to date........................148 miles
Total time in saddle to date............11hrs 23mins
Average speed for trip to date..............13mph

Day Three: Westward Ho! to Bridgwater

or, The One Where Tony Hits the Heights (and the Shops)

A reasonable night's sleep all things considered, but I was up at six o'clock with thoughts running through my head about how best to tackle the problem in hand - re-checking of websites and route cards didn't do much to settle me!

After getting up and having a cup of tea the hostel owner advised me of a bike shop in Bideford (pronounced Biddy-ford, random English coastal town fans) that should be able to sort me out.

Rather than cycle over there then back, I thought I'd give them a call and see if she was right. A quick google and I was on the phone to Freebird. Speaking to the owner he let me know he couldn't sort me out with a rack and panniers ('we *used* to stock that sort') but they had '*hundreds* of backpacks including some specific cycling ones'. I asked what sort, but he suggested going to look. Hopeful, I set off...

What a load of squit! His 'cycling specific' bag (yes, bag...singular!) was a printed US Postal Cycling Team cloth musette! As for the others, suitable for a stroll around town but not a hundred mile journey to Bristol!

Slightly peeved (to put it mildly!) I headed out and onto the road for the four mile or so journey back to Atlantic City - the lovely downhill into Westward Ho! the night before wasn't quite as much fun in the opposite direction. The headwind only adding to the occasion...although it did mean I'd benefit from a favourable tailwind during the day ahead!

I got to the outlet village, parked the bike up outside a massive ASDA and wandered into Mountain Warehouse. After perusing the massive range of options (that's hundreds of bags, Mr. Freebird!) I opted for a 10ltr pack, bought it and got ready to set off.

It was now 11.00 and realising I hadn't eaten I slipped into the ASDA and settled into the cafe with a Full Monty breakfast. Whilst eating, my situation hit me. Ten days to go and I'd encountered a problem that I'd never even considered would occur. It took a moment to convince myself that I'd manage fine but I got myself back on track, finished off my breakfast and set back out to return to the hostel.

After arriving I shifted all my stuff from the Carradice into the rucksack - hmm...it was a tight fit, maybe the bigger one would have been better!

Off came the broken rack and into the Carradice bag it went. 'What did you do with that as you said your rucksack's full?' I hear you cry...well, I pootled into Westward Ho!, found the Post Office, packaged it up and sent it back home where it will wait until I get back to return to its maker alongside an, erm, strongly worded letter!

Finally on the road at 12.15ish (so much for those early starts!) and after tackling the steep climb out of Ho! I joined the A39 headed towards Barnstaple. It became apparent very quickly that the bag wasn't working, and there was no way I'd cope with another ninety five miles or so. A new plan was needed, so I pulled over to the verge and got on the iPhone.

A google for 'Barnstaple cycle shops' threw back three promising results. The Bike Shed's response to my request for a seatpost rack and panniers for a road bike without eyelets wasn't inspiring; 'er, I'm sure we could fashion something together' so I decided to try the next one, Planet Bike, who simply said 'yep, no worries'. Sold!

I put their postcode into my GPS and made my way across the ten miles or so into Barnstaple proper, arriving in an industrial estate where hopefully I'd get myself sorted...

What can I say? Paul and Neil at Planet Bike were superb, my heroes for the day! Within minutes I had

a new, secure, rack fitted and no more than twenty minutes later I had my stuff transferred over to a new bag. It turns out that Paul did a LEJOG with his twin brother last year, so I had a bit of a chat. I knew the day would be tough, his sucking of teeth and nervous laughter did nothing but confirm that! After looking at my route for the day he joyfully exclaimed I was in for a hell of a climb with a 'terrific Cat. I effort' for the first hill of the day. Oh joy...

The final 'pep talk' from Paul as I bid them farewell cheered me up no end; 'I'm envious of you, a great two weeks ahead. Get through today and you'll be fine, Scotland's easy after this!'.

Pulling away from the estate with the weight back on the bike was amazing. Planet Bike I salute you and kiss you on both cheeks! It was now worryingly 14.00 and I had sixty miles still to cover. And that climb...

A ride through town towards Snapper and the climb started. Dear God, what a climb! As I reached about three quarters of the way up I passed Bratton Fleming. Stopping for an ice cream at the village stores I had a chat with the owner. After telling him where I was off to, his reply of 'another one?! You all come in here' tickled me as I imagined the state that some may be in at that point of the ascent. He assured me there wasn't much further to go which, whilst a little bit of a lie, did cheer me up!

The road finally peaked and levelled onto Exmoor National Park. With the road to myself and the sun beating down on fields strewn with sheep and lambs I had a chance to reflect on the journey so far - a hawk (kestrel perhaps) bathing in the sun literally yards away only added to the experience.

There were a couple more ups and downs before I reached Wheddon Cross where the road plummets and winds through woodlands. What a thrill, a lovely reward for the struggle at the start of the day and I

really enjoyed the descent, despite the chill that the shadows of the trees cast onto the road.

Twenty miles 'til Bridgwater, but being back on a main road (A39) gave me a chance to make some time up. One spell in particular was magical, sweeping curves at a decent speed with the Atlantic in full view and the sun setting behind me...breathtaking. I rolled into the B&B as the sun set around 21.00. A long old day.

I'm sure you're desperate to know, but I've no idea what the state of Bridgwater's fish and chips are like. With a lovely kitchen available in the B&B I took full advantage and used it to cook...an oven pizza!

So in conclusion. A long, long day both physically and mentally...but so satisfying as I made it to Bridgwater. Here's hoping for a better day tomorrow, with ninety miles to cover and a trip over the Severn. Toodles!

Stats for Monday 17th May 2010

Distance..86 miles
Time in saddle...6hrs 26mins
Average speed..13.3mph
Maximum speed........ ....39.9mph (gah!)

Total distance to date..234 miles
Total time in saddle to date............ ....17hrs 49mins
Average speed for trip to date............ ....13.1mph

Tuesday 18th May 2010

Day Four: Bridgwater to Hereford

or, The One Where It All Started Creaking

A less stressful start to the day, although I didn't get out of the B&B until gone ten o'clock. I've settled into the habit of jotting down notes about the day for the blog in the evening and then writing it up properly and in full after getting up in the morning. In theory this should stop you having to read a blog strewn with errors caused by drowsiness!

Anyway, once on the road I made good progress with a well-surfaced, undulating thirty miles or so to start the day. I stopped half way into this stretch to pick up some supplies, and having noticed a slight niggle in my inner right thigh, got some stretches in.

As the road started climbing for the first time I passed a pub with a board outside offering a mid-week meal deal for a fiver...

Forty minutes, a cheeseburger, apple pie and custard and a Pepsi later and I was back on the road. Sixty miles still to go and it was already two o'clock. In my head I gave myself a mental 'deadline' of eight o'clock to get myself to the B&B and gave them a call to let them know my planned arrival time (well, it's only good manners isn't it?!).

I noticed as I set on my way that my left pedal was creaking slightly - nothing to worry about really, anyone that uses LOOK pedals will know they have a tendency to do this. I made a note to get it sorted when I passed a bike shop...bit of grease should do it.

The miles were passing steadily and although the surfaces were nowhere near as good as I'd experienced to date, I made my way through Bristol; the cycleway following along the gorgeous Avon Gorge which looked incredible in the late-May sunshine.

Bristol came and went and I carried along the approach to the Severn Bridge. After what

seemed like miles and miles I made it to the bridge and set about crossing it - cycles allowed down the side of the bridge upon a path which is also used as a maintenance roadway.

Got to be honest...I didn't like it. I'm not a huge fan of heights and, as I stopped to take a photo, the way in which it bounces around as trucks rumble past is really unnerving!

Back on terra firma and a slight misreading of the map took me about a quarter of a mile off course, up a road and towards a Tesco Express. Whilst this gave me a chance to stock up, I also had the opportunity to treat myself to a spell of time in what's easily the 'scummiest' area I've seen so far!

Leaving behind the kids in their Corsas and their groupies in the Tesco car park was a tough thing to do but I had to crack on...sorry guys.

Remember that creaking pedal? Well it had got worse. It's not a nice 'eek eek' mousy squeak either. Oh no, it's a full on plastic-y 'crrk crrk' and I reckon I can be heard for a good half mile or so as I, literally, grind myself onwards - must find a bike shop...

The latter part of the day is where the hills started. There was a few peaks which, although no way near as bad as that one yesterday, were still testing and that niggle in my leg was getting more noticeable and seemingly spreading around the leg.

Fifteen miles to go and I pulled out the knee brace that I'd packed last minute and put that on the troublesome leg - I'm not a huge fan of supports, and firmly believe they should be a last resort... but needs must. It did the trick and the pain eased enough to carry on at a reasonable pace.

The final four miles or so was a lovely downhill stretch and was needed after what had turned

into a bit of a slog. I eventually found the B&B at nine o'clock, having first of all gone completely the wrong way (bloody GPS had been set incorrectly!).

A wander to the nearby Sainsbury's to pick up some tea (honey and mustard chicken pasta, orange juice and a For Goodness Shakes strawberry milkshake) and some frozen vegetables to use as an ice pack on my right leg (classy!).

A quick google has thrown up a bike shop nearby that looks good, a proper local one - so a trip there early doors tomorrow to sort out the creaking, then on my way to Chester. A hundred miles, reckon that's a good ten hours...

Finally, a big thank you to everyone that's been in touch (be it by text, phone or online) - it's nice to know that there's someone out there reading my ramblings. Thanks also to everybody that's sponsored me so far, it really is appreciated and is another factor that's keeping me motivated.

Stats for Tuesday 18ᵗʰ May 2010

Distance..94 miles
Time in saddle......................................7hrs 9mins
Average speed.......................................13.0mph
Maximum speed..................................46.0mph (eek!)

Total distance to date......................328 miles
Total time in saddle to date............24hrs 58mins
Average speed for trip to date..........13.1mph

Wednesday 19th May 2010

Day Five: Hereford to Chester

*or, The One Where Tony Gets Lubed and Sticks it in the Little Ring for the Day**

Up reasonably early and over to Coombes Cycles by 09.15 to try and sort out the incessant squeaking. The guy working there, Mark, was also a user of LOOK pedals and had a chuckle with me as he sorted out my problem with a bit of grease. He also kindly tightened up my bottom bracket (ooo-er!) and pedals which had worked themselves a little loose. All of this was done free of charge. What a guy!

Bit of a dull day scenery wise, but then what more can you expect when the route consists of sixty five miles on the A49, a bit of the A5, back onto the A49 and then a few other smaller A-roads into Chester itself?

So yeah, boring in terms of views but seduce a mallard it was a quick one - helped no end by the fact there were no silly climbs and the road undulated perfectly for the majority of the trip. Here comes the science bit, concentrate...

undulating *(un-joo-lay-ting)*; adj.

1. Moving up and down like waves; wavy
2. Forming a series of regular curves

Now, whilst I was doing my preparation for the marathon (ha...listen to me, the 'athlete'!), hearing a route described as this was the last thing I wanted. Slight inclines are hard when you're running, but ideal on a bike. Bear with me...

Steep hills are bad, obviously; and quick descents, although fun, are over far too quickly. A flat surface may sound ideal, but requires constant effort so is more tiring than it appears which leaves undulating.

This gives you a chance to work on the slight inclines and relax on the downward sloping bits. And if you could have taken the traffic off the roads today, it would have been cycling nirvana...!

With my leg and knee giving me some gyp the day before I spent the day with my knee brace on and concentrated on ensuring I was 'spinning' the gears as opposed to 'mashing' them - spinning means keeping the gears in the lower chainring and therefore getting more revolutions in at a higher speed. If you 'mash' the gears you usually have the gears on the big chainring and really push through...putting much more pressure on your knees and legs.

So I stayed in the little chainring all day and my knee felt a lot better for it, which is a good thing!

With favourable conditions and a decent route for the day I arrived into Chester at 18.30...woo, early for once!

I booked myself into the hostel for the night (just me and one other this time, very quiet!) and nipped out to grab some tea. Once again there was a kitchen available to use so I decided to be a bit more adventurous this time and opted for chicken pizza (Poultry? On a pizza?! Crazy!), some jam doughnuts and banana milk for a change...it's like being a child again this trip!

Quick update to finish off, as I've been asked a few questions to date...

'How's the arse?' - I can happily report no chafing issues to date (Assos Chamois Cream. Mmm... tingly!), although my sit bones are starting to complain if the road surface deteriorates...who'd have thought that would happen, hey?!

'Got a silly tan yet?' - yep, it's started. Nice lines where the cycling top sleeves end and nice white hands where the gloves are. Amusingly, it's more noticeable on the right arm, but then I guess that's where the sun is as I'm cycling. Not burnt though...hurrah!

'Did you pay a toll at the Severn Bridge?' - nope, bikes are free. Wouldn't recommend it though. Especially if you don't like heights!

'How are you securing your bike?' - I actually think you'd be okay without one, as I'm rarely more than ten yards away, but I did pack a coil lock. Will update the kit list later.

'Have you met any other cyclists?' - going my way, until Bristol, no. Even then they were only out on a short run or commuting. Today though I saw my first group of LEJOG-ers, a small peleton of four first of all passed me as I was on my phone on the side of the climb out of Hereford.

We obviously took different routes as, sixty five miles later I was on the side of the road on my phone and they passed me again...who knows what they think of me! Anyway, I chatted to their support vehicle and found out they're due in John O'Groats late next week (Their blog is at http://www.bmfend2end2010.com/ if you fancy seeing how a group does it). Good luck guys!

'How are you feeling?' - pretty positive actually. It's a bit odd only having one thing to focus on for the day and as bizarre as it sounds, knowing you've 'only' got to cover 'x' miles before the sun sets is strangely relaxing. I've had a lot of time to think!

Thanks for reading so far. I know Ive said it before, but it really is nice to know that I'm not simply rambling for no reason (does a blog with no readers make a sound?!).

Off to Morecambe tomorrow. Seaside fish and chips and a photo with that statue methinks...!

* Snigger. Oh, come on...you must have at least smirked?!

Stats for Wednesday 19th May 2010

Distance..94 miles (again!)
Time in saddle....................................6hrs 28mins
Average speed....................................14.5mph
Maximum speed................................36.4mph

Total distance to date....................................422 miles
Total time in saddle to date............ ....31hrs 26mins
Average speed for trip to date......................13.4mph

Day Six: Chester to Morecambe

or, The One Where Tony Buys Daphne Some Rings...

Made the decision last night to wash all my cycling clothes and leave them to dry as I slept...

Of course they were still wet when I woke up with the intention of an early start - hmm, must remember not to do that again! Anyway, problem to solve...clothes to dry. I packed everything into a bag and set out looking for launderette nearby with a tumble drier.

Nipping into the nearby newsagents to ask if they knew of one, the two ladies in there told me 'no' before one of them said 'what is it you need to dry?'. I explained it was just some cycling bits and was surprised to hear her reply of, 'bring it back to mine, I'm just round the corner. I'll do it for you'!

So round to Dorothy's house I went with Max (her Yorkie), where she put my wet cycling clothes in the drier - before suggesting I get out for breakfast and come back when it would be done. So off I went to Wetherspoons...

A large breakfast later and I was on the way back. Walking past a cycle shop I nipped in to see if I could get some grease off them in a bit to try and put a stop to the creaking pedals. No worries, brilliant.

Collecting my now dry clothes from Dorothy and thanking her for her hospitality (how kind of her!) I set off to the hostel to pack up and get my bike to the shop for that dab of grease...

Well, I told Ellis at The Edge Cycleworks the problem and after a quick look he informed me I was in fact missing a crank bolt and the noise was the crank wobbling. Bugger.

Unfortunately he didn't have a part in place that would make do (and it would be a make do, not permanent) and whilst a bodge could be done, he couldn't guarantee it would last long at all - and

certainly not for another six hundred miles. I was planning on upgrading the bike anyway at some point in the future, just not quite so soon...but with the threat of a crank snapping off at some point soon I thought it was as good a time as any.

One hour later and Daphne was fully upgraded with a new crankset, rear cassette and chain. Having seen the old crank it was definitely something that needed doing, a gouge in the side indicating just where that noise was coming from every pedal turn.

Thank you to Ellis for fitting me in at short, short notice and for giving the bike a quick tune up in the process. Good luck with your singlespeed LEJOG next year...you're mental!

So, on the road at 12.00ish (so much for the early starts!) and my wallet was lighter, but the bike was certainly running smoothly. It was strange hearing nothing as I was pedalling! Yes, it was another odd start to the day but at least it makes for a more entertaining blog, hey...?!

A solid day of cycling, into a slight northerly headwind for much of the day. Nothing particularly of note as I passed through villages, although the roads were quieter than the last couple of days which made for a far more pleasant journey.

With twenty five miles to go I pulled into a garage for a feed stop. As I started to tuck into my strawberry yoghurt drink (I swear I picked up a milkshake!) a familiar face strolled up. Richard, a friend from football had been waiting with his daughter Sophie for me to appear on the A6! It was good to have a bit of a chat, and thanks once again to him and her for taking the time out of their day to see me...much appreciated!

A bit further up the road there was a local cycling club hosting a ten mile time trial event. Of course, had I not been fully loaded and already completed

seventy miles for the day I'd have blitzed the field... instead I simply admired their pace as the pairs zipped past at regular intervals. Chapeau!

With about ten miles to go I passed someone walking his laden bike with a flat rear tire. Stopping to ask if I could help he explained he was staying at a campsite just up the road, but thanked me for asking.

After a short chat (his tip; NEVER take camping kit, it's a pain in the f*cking arse up hills!) he said he was heading up to 'the top' and was due the same time as me. I wished him well and suggested we maybe meet to have a laugh about it all over a beer then.

I sailed through Lancaster on a lovely descending road. It looks really pretty and I couldn't help but think it would have been a nice stop - shame there was no cheap accommodation available.

I arrived into Morecambe at about quarter past nine after completing the last four miles or so on a lovely cycle path. Have to tell you, Morecambe's not nice...and it definitely needs investment. Imagine a cheap version of Blackpool and you'd not be far off!

Tea was courtesy of Tesco again - hot cross buns, a blueberry muffin and strawberry milk (for a change!). I treated myself to a bottle of...Deep Heat (!) and drifted off to sleep in the glow of that, dreaming of tomorrow and the big climb...

Stats for Thursday 20th May 2010

Distance	95 miles
Time in saddle	6hrs 51mins
Average speed	13.8mph
Maximum speed	28.3mph

Total distance to date	517 miles
Total time in saddle to date	30hrs 17mins
Average speed for trip to date	13.5mph

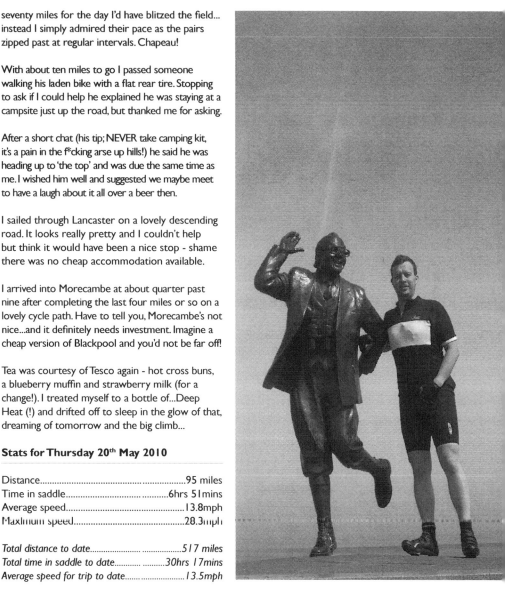

Friday 21st May 2010

Day Seven: Morecambe to Carlisle

or, The One With the Pass

It's a strange old place to be, in the saddle of the bicycle for days at a time. You have the freedom that no other road user can ever dream of having and are more or less in total control with how you want to travel; you can travel for miles and miles in a carefree state with your legs ticking over effortlessly and then, in the same hour in some cases, every pedal stroke is torture and that saddle feels like the loneliest place on the planet as you try and plough through.

No point beating round the bush...today was tough. Tougher than my first century back to Peterborough. Tougher than that day through Exmoor earlier on this tour. It was, by far, the toughest day I have EVER had on two wheels!

Finally finished writing Day Six's blog and got out of the B&B at around 10.45 (so much for the early starts!), setting off on the coastal road out of Morecambe - stopping for the obligatory photo with Eric, of course. The couple that kindly took my photo also gave me some sponsorship money too, after I explained what I was doing...thank you!

The first twenty five miles were great cycling miles with decent surfaces and lovely terrain. The first five miles or so along the coast were particularly nice, with the sea breeze offering a nice respite to the already warm sun.

I stopped for a feed stop in Ings (best flapjack in the world!) and had a chat with the guy in the shop. He commented on my route as we chatted; 'so you're going over the Pass?!', 'yep', 'good luck with that!'. Gulp!

After another twenty five miles the hills started, gentle at first before it appeared...

...'Kirkstone Pass 5'. Looks pretty innocuous like that, doesn't it? What that sign doesn't tell you

is that it's a long, winding road up the side of the fells. Yes, it's pretty...but there's nothing up there. Nothing. Not even a McDonalds and they're everywhere (actually, that's a lie...I haven't seen many golden arches at all on this trip)!

Just me, my bike, this god awful road, the beating sun and sheep. Lots of sheep. Seems to be the 'in thing' up here, sheep. They're nice and everything, but they don't offer much encouragement when you stop at the side of the road. At least a cow would sound like it was telling you to 'moo-ve'...

I digress. As I (slowly) wound my way up the climb I remembered my Garmin wasn't the base model...mine had an altimeter built in! Now, it took just as long and I seemed to be stopping for far longer than I was actually cycling but the numbers slowly ticked over...500ft, 600ft, 700ft, 800ft, 900ft, 850ft (oh yes, there were slight dips too...just for giggles I guess), 900ft, 1,000ft, 1,100ft, 1,200ft, 1,300ft, 1,400ft, 1,450ft...

Then, as I rounded another bend, I saw it. A pub! That must be the summit, you wouldn't build a pub called The Kirkstone Inn before the top would you?! I powered (ha!) up the final few yards to 1,500ft and as the road levelled out I knew. I'd done it. I'd f*cking done it!

Not sure what the guy in the blue top thought as a hot, sweaty but deleriously happy cyclist thrust a camera at him but I wanted a photo! Thanking him, he told me to enjoy the descent...'it's worth that climb'.

As I sat at the top and pondered what I'd just done, the support vehicle for that group I mentioned the other day rolled in. He kindly filled up my bidon with water (so much water...that's where a support vehicle comes in handy!) and we had a bit of a chat on how things were going.

Stats for Friday 21st May 2010

Distance...82 miles
Time in saddle......................................6hrs 20mins
Average speed...13.0mph
Maximum speed.......................................34.8mph

Total distance to date.........................599 miles (gah!)
Total time in saddle to date............ ....44hrs 37mins
Average speed for trip to date...........................13.4mph

We'll probably see each other en route again but if not, and you are reading this...good luck.

Setting off over the flat summit I indulged myself a little with a small arms aloft celebration, Le Tour style. Yes, I probably looked ridiculous but I'm never going to win a polka dot jersey...let me be Contador for just one minute!

You'd think the descent would be fun but it wasn't to start with! Twenty per cent (that's one in five, fraction fans!) descents round hairpin curves aren't for the faint hearted. Use of the brakes had my rims red hot in minutes and I had to stop to let them cool for fear of bursting an inner tube! After a while it levels out a bit and the meandering curves with the peaks and lakes in view are breathtaking. I stopped for a break at Pattersdale (best brownie ever!) and set off again.

Now, the Garmin has this lovely 'feature' that is the knack of turning itself off as the road gets too bumpy (fair enough). As I rounded the lake I realised it had done so and turned it back on to find I'd missed a subtle turn off. Two and a half miles back. I cheerfully (ha!) pedalled my way back to this point and got going in the right direction to hit the second climb of the day. This one was 'only' 600ft according to my route card but my legs were refusing to oblige.

I laboured my way up this tortuous climb, my legs burning with every stroke and somehow made it to the top. No celebrations this time out, just a real desire to get the last thirty miles or so out of the way so I could get some rest.

The last spell of the journey along desolate local roads flew by in comparison, and I arrived at the Arkale Lodge in Carlisle at around 20.15.

Pat welcomed me in and informed me he was entertaining his daughter-in-law Georgina and grandchildren (Niamh and Grace) for the weekend. I apologised for the late arrival and hoped I hadn't ruined any evening plans for them - the food that was being cooked smelt delicious.

With the heat throwing up dust and grime from the roads I asked if it would be possible for me to use a tumble drier to dry off clothes if I rinsed them. I was amazed when Pat said he'd do better than that and would wash and dry them for me...thank you!

After showering it was time for food. Whilst there was a Burger King over the road, I felt like something a bit more substantial so asked if they could recommend anywhere nearby.

Pat said I could join them! Not only was he kind enough to offer to do my washing, he was going to feed me too! Feeling guilty I asked again (and again) if he was sure, but he insisted. American ranch chilli chicken, rice and carrots. And peaches and ice cream for dessert. I could have cried, dear reader. We shot the breeze over the meal, topics including travel, Las Vegas and British seaside towns. It was a really nice end to what had been a struggle of a day.

So it was off to bed with a hearty meal inside me for a change and thoughts of tomorrow's trip into Scotland and up to Edinburgh already forcing the struggle of today out of my mind.

Reflecting on the day just gone I thought of the towns I'd been through (Kendal and Windemere in particular were lovely), the sights I'd seen (RAF fighter planes tearing round the peaks a particular highlight) and the stories that I'd have to tell once I get home. I started to think that it's not all bad I guess, it's almost enjoyable in a weird way.

It's a strange old place to be, in the saddle of the bicycle for days at a time...

Saturday 22nd May 2010

Day Eight: Carlisle to Edinburgh

or, The One on the A7

After a terrific breakfast at the Arkale Lodge (I really would recommend it to anyone heading up to Carlisle), I was on the road by 09.40...yay! It took a while to get out of the city, thanks to a funny one way system and a liberal smattering of traffic lights that seemed intent on changing to red as I approached.

Finally on the A7 out of Carlisle, I noticed a sign; 'Edinburgh 95'. Now, my route was meant to take me a more direct ninety miles but after yesterday's 'fun and games' with local roads and a northerly headwind settling in (so much for seasonal prevailing south westerlies!), I made the decision to main road it all day.

And main road it I did. Practically all of the ninety five miles on the A7! It wasn't easy, mind. There's not that many settlements on the Scottish side of the border, and service stations are just as rare - certainly not as many as on English trunk roads, so it was a case of taking advantage when I did see them.

And the sun. Oh, the sun. I hope those of you reading enjoyed your day in it, 'cos it was unbearable at times on the bike...relentless from above and after midday you could feel it coming back up off the tarmac.

The first ten miles were hard work. Getting into a rhythm wasn't happening and it took a while to get going. After a while it clicked though and I got through to the halfway point just as I hit Hawick.

Apparently the home of cashmere, Hawick is also the proud owner of a big Morrison's which I decided would do for lunch. I took a good break in the sun, phoning home for a chat and a progress update. I probably took too big a break actually; that climb back out of Hawick would have been tough anyway, but my legs just didn't want to turn. It was a good distance until I felt properly on my way again.

The A7 is quite pretty as far as main roads go, winding it's way round the green, green hills and dales but a pretty strong headwind picked up later on into the day...not something I really needed for the last twenty miles or so!

The last five miles will probably go down as the worst five on my trip. Edinburgh's traffic system borders on the ridiculous! Terrible road surfaces and cycling into a sun so low I may as well have had my eyes closed I cursed my way to the final point on my Garmin which turned out to not be where I was staying - another mistaken input by me, d'oh! It couldn't find the place I wanted so it was a slow, painful drag to the right place checking my iPhone for references at random junction stops.

My bed for tonight is courtesy of Caledonian Backpackers, which describes itself as a hostel but is in fact more a cross between Byker Grove and a bunkhouse (equipped with a bar, games room and 'cinema area'). I'm sure if you're here as a group, or for a spell of nights, it's wonderful...I'm just hoping I manage to get a reasonable night's sleep in.

A trip to nearby Somerfield and I picked up some malt loaf and milk for tea. As I re-joined the street littered with drunk revellers (perhaps planning on stopping in Edinburgh on a Saturday night wasn't the best plan...) it hit me just quite how much I didn't want to be in a busy city right now! Wandering down Princes Street with my two pints of strawberry milk, I've never felt so out of place. I'm a city boy, give me hustle and bustle any day of the week and I'm usually fine with it...but having had eight days on the road all I want at the moment is a comfy bed for the night!

It was back into the still empty hostel room for the night; so you'll have to wait until tomorrow to see if my room mates are up to Westward Ho!'s standard, I'm afraid. Into deeper Scotland and onto Crianlarich tomorrow and back to a 'real' SYHA run hostel which is hopefully a damn sight quieter...

Stats for Saturday 22nd May 2010

Distance...95 miles
Time in saddle...................................7hrs 14mins
Average speed.....................................13.1mph
Maximum speed..................................37.9mph

Total distance to date..........................694 miles
Total time in saddle to date..............51hrs 51mins
Average speed for trip to date................13.4mph

Sunday 23rd May 2010

Day Nine: Edinburgh to Crianlarich

or, The One Where Tony Gets Wind

Well...whilst I didn't formally get introduced to my 'roomies', they made sure I was aware of their presence as they stumbled back into the hostel at half past one in the morning. Sigh.

Actually, that's a bit harsh. There were five others in the room I left in the morning - it was just the three Australians that created the hullabaloo. No, really. Australians. Being loud. I'm shocked too...

Anyway...two of them came, sorry, stumbled in first. I think they were boyfriend and girlfriend, but only because they were in the same bed as I was leaving. They chatted for a bit before their mate Jason came in with what must have been twenty pounds worth of McDonalds which took him half an hour to eat.

The couple were amazed at their drunken state as they'd 'only drunk half as much as last night', although I'd be tempted to agree with their conclusion that, yes, it probably was 'the five Jaeger-Bombs at the start' that ruined them.

They got off to sleep or, more accurately, passed out, as Jason moved onto his apple pie (who buys a McDonalds apple pie when under the influence?!). The girl, in a style only Antipodeans can really pull off, slumped half out of the bed with her head in the bin as she thought she was 'gonna hurl'. Well done buddy, she's a keeper!

Enough about them, this is supposed to be about the journey! I was up at six o'clock to take advantage of the 'simple breakfast' they offer. Simple it was, but the self-service tea, toast and cornflakes was very welcome.

There were a fair number of people in running kit up and about and, after enquiring, I found out it was the day of the Edinburgh marathon. Now, whilst this explains the difficulty I had in finding

somewhere in the city to stay for the night and the odd road closures, I've not got a clue as to why on Earth you'd prepare yourself for a marathon with a night at Caledonian Backpackers?!

Anyway...I was up and out of the room and ready to get going by half past seven (so much for the earl...oh!). As if to mock my calling for more bearable weather yesterday a cool rain was falling as I battled against Edinburgh's seemingly random road network once again as I looked to join the Forth Road Bridge.

After ten miles of back roads ('cos you're not allowed on the A70 on your bike...which they don't tell you 'til you get to it!) I reached the bridge and admired the view...

Or not. A real 'pea souper' had enveloped the structure with visibility no more than two hundred yards which was a shame.

As the day wore on and the sun came out it burnt the water off the road surface - eerie 'smoke' peeling up and off the tarmac as I clocked through the miles.

The journey was a good one, with reasonable road surfaces for the majority of the day (some dreadful ones too though; really jarring, despite the carbon forks and seatpost designed to dampen those sort of bumps).

I passed through some lovely little towns and got to see some amazing scenery. Circling Loch Lubnaig, with the mountains in the background and the sun glistening off the water's surface was picture postcard perfect and I couldn't help but think how lucky I was to be seeing it in the way I was...a way so few people are lucky enough to do so, with car journeys giving the passenger far less time to savour the scenery.

I got towards the end of the journey for the day and it all went a little squiffy. Remember that head wind I've mentioned before? Well it returned, this time with a vengeance. The last twenty miles was going to be bad enough with a six hundred foot climb to take on but the headwind made it far, far worse...I was crawling along at 8mph for spells, literally being held up in the wind!

If anybody up there is looking down on me can I please have some southerlies for the rest of the week? Or none at all! Just not any more northerlies, pur-lease!

Despite the struggle of the last twenty miles or so, with the early start I'd managed to get it was nice to take a look down at the GPS and see it displaying 3.50 miles to go as opposed to 35.0 come the time four o'clock rolled round! An early finish for the day (yay!) as I arrived into my stop for the night.

Crianlarich is a lovely little village in the shadow of a couple of huge mountains (I'm calling them mountains, the locals probably think of them as mere slopes). I grabbed dinner in the local pub, venison burger and chips followed by apple tart and custard. It was excellent.

The hostel is exactly what I was expecting, full of walkers and people here to enjoy the area rather than the bars and clubs within it. Should get a good night's sleep in here, no worries. I love it!

Only problem though is that there's no signal on the o2 mobile phone network anywhere so I've had to update the blog via the hostel's extortionate wi-fi network (one pound for twenty minutes?! That's obscene!). I have a feeling this'll be the case for much of the rest of my journey so I'm hoping there's

somewhere in Loch Ness, Tongue and finally at the finish in John O'Groats that I'm able to do the same. So...if you are trying to get hold of me and I don't answer, that'll probably be the reason why!

It's a bit scary to think I'm now three quarters of the way through this trip and I'm down to less than three hundred miles (in theory!) until I cross that finish line. Or, more childishly...

...three more sleeps! On to Loch Ness tomorrow (just need to follow one road again!), and if I manage another early start and get the tricky first half of the journey done quickly enough I should have time for a bit of Nessie hunting!

Stats for Sunday 23rd May 2010

Distance...84 miles
Time in saddle.................................6hrs 31mins
Average speed....................................12.8mph
Maximum speed.................................34.3mph

Total distance to date................................778 miles
Total time in saddle to date............58hrs 22mins
Average speed for trip to date........................13.3mph

Monday 24th May 2010

Day Ten: Crianlarich to Loch Ness

or, The One With the Invisible Hindrance(s)

After a decent night's sleep it was another relatively early start to the day and I was out on the road (and the only road for the day!) by half past eight. Before nine o'clock two days running?! Woo woo!

Before leaving the hostel in Crianlarich I'd taken the opportunity to look at the mountaineering weather report. Disappointingly, it forecasted north or north westerly winds; up to 15mph. Damn you weather Gods!

A relatively flat first five miles got my legs ticking over quite nicely. I started to think that perhaps it wouldn't be such a bad day after all and I could be at Loch Ness by half five.

Then I turned a corner and hit the wind. And the first climb of the day. Just what you want at the same time! After struggling my way up, the road rounded a corner; trees offering shelter from the wind. It was here I noticed the chill in the air and stopped to get my leg warmers out...no point being cold all day!

As the road dropped the views were spectacular. High peaks all around and valleys plunging down to pools of water. It was all very Jurassic Park like, and I really wouldn't have been shocked if I'd seen a herd of Diplodocus grazing in the distance...

I didn't of course. That would be silly. Although it's so unpopulated up in the Highlands there could be that happening just over the next mountain and nobody would be any the wiser!

Back up to a thousand feet and across a desolate moor offering no shelter whatsoever, the wind was picking up. I've got used to putting effort in on the inclines but pedalling downhill?! I didn't sign up to that!

It was on the descent back down to sea level that I hit a crack in the road that I simply did not see at all. The jolt through the bike and the handlebars was shocking, and I'm pretty sure my yelp of pain was probably heard back in Edinburgh (similar to that of a dog if you tread on its tail, if you were wondering...).

The shock was bad enough but it was the 'clank clank clank' sound that I heard afterwards that worried me more. Stopping to have a look I saw that I'd managed to break a spoke...

With a bodge the spoke held in place, but with the wheel already slightly out of true I realised I was going to get another opportunity to see inside a bike shop. Sigh.

I carried onwards, scanning the road surface ahead with eagle eyes - the last thing I needed was to hit another bump and have the wheel collapse on me...that would be a disaster!

Around fifteen miles later I reached Glencoe and, as if by chance, saw a sign at the side of the road advertising cycle hire and repairs. No answer on the phone, but there was an address so I went searching.

Found the place (not too hard, most of these places are pretty small up here!) just as the proprietor arrived back on his bike...which explains why he didn't answer the phone. Unfortunately he didn't have any road bike wheel spokes in stock, but recommended I try Nevis Bikes up in Fort William. After looking at the damage he cheerfully exclaimed; 'aye, that'll hold. It's only sixteen miles or so'.

Stopping at the village store for some food, I gave Nevis Cycles a call and explained my predicament. They said they were busy but should be able to fit me in as I was heading in this trip.

I made good time reaching Fort William (still scanning the road surface ahead!) and left my bike in the hands of Joe as I went off for a wander.

On returning, his opening sentence of 'you have a small problem' made my heart drop, before he followed up with 'we only had silver spokes so you've now got an odd one' and my heartbeat levelled out...!

I thanked him for fitting me in at such short notice and got on my way, the unplanned stops having added around an hour onto my day.

After setting off from Fort William I somehow made good time despite the head wind that was picking up once again. Whether it was because I'm getting fitter as the back to back days continue or simply because I was desperate to finish for the day I don't know but I got to the hostel at half past six...only an hour later than I'd thought I would as I set off for the day.

The place is lovely, but very basic. I somehow secured myself a solo room (with a Loch view!), which is a bonus in regards to getting some quality sleep. It's also another opportunity to apply some Deep Heat overnight in an attempt to keep my legs ticking over nicely.

Tea was a Soreen Malt Loaf with strawberry milk...what a mature diet, and, after a wander down to the 'beach' for a few photos, I spent a while in the common room overlooking the Loch chatting to other residents for the night.

Now I'm nearing the end of my journey (wow, first time I've got to say that!) and the route you can take is less variable than at the start I'm starting to see a few more cyclists.

There's been a couple heading southwards and there's four in this hostel (three older guys, one solo and a pair, who are doing it over three weeks unsupported; and a Scouse guy with his mate as support who's doing it over seven days and is

finishing tomorrow! To be fair, he does triathlons for fun and has finished the Ironman. Twice!).

Tomorrow's also the big one for me. Up to Tongue and with the twenty mile an hour northerlies that have been predicted, I think it's going to be a day of hard work...

A liberal application of Deep Heat before bed and I was soon drifting off with a children's television programme ditty rolling round inside my head as it had been for a while approaching Loch Ness...

You can knock it,
You can rock it,
You can go to Timbuktu,
But you'll never find a Nessie in the zoo!

Stats for Monday 24th May 2010

Distance	94 miles
Time in saddle	7hrs 2mins
Average speed	13.3mph
Maximum speed	29.8mph

Total distance to date	872 miles
Total time in saddle to date	65hrs 24mins
Average speed for trip to date	13.3mph

Day Eleven: Loch Ness to Tongue

or, The One Where Tony Done a Ton (sic.)

Like a boxer winning on points after twelve rounds, plucky underdogs clinging on to a one goal lead having had a man sent off or a runner hitting the final six miles of a marathon in thirty plus degrees heat...today was a slog.

I'd anticipated it was going to be like that, of course. It wasn't particularly tough...I got through it without any niggles, it was just hard work. For a long time. A very long time.

Knowing I was in for a 'fun' day, if only for the distance, I was up and out of the hostel early having had a breakfast of currant buns and strawberry milk that I'd picked up the night before a few miles out from the hostel ('cos it really is remote at the Loch Ness hostel, there's nothing around it!).

It was nice to be on the road by half past seven and the first thirty miles or so flew by, with the tree-lined A82 offering excellent shelter from the wind.

About five miles down the road a deer jumped out of the trees and ran in front of me for about a mile before darting back into the undergrowth. Having spotted it coming it was quite a sight to behold, but it was easy to see how they can cause a nuisance to cars.

Reaching Inverness and looking at the Cateye as I stopped to pick up some supplies (shortbread as a snack...well, I've got to get something Scottish!), I was amazed to see I'd averaged 14.9mph! I knew it wasn't going to last, unfortunately...

And, lo, once out of Inverness the weather Gods were awoken. And they sent unto he the winds of wrath. Okay, maybe a big dramatic but it certainly felt like that once I turned to head north proper.

Anyone that's read my blog in it's entirety will have read about my trip back to Peterborough. For

those that haven't (and I don't blame you!), I made a trip back to 'boro on Easter Sunday which was a similar distance and into a headwind the whole trip. Today was like that. Only with a stronger headwind. And hillier. Peterborough and the surrounding area isn't renound for its rolling countryside!

They big hill in the middle of the route (I forget it's name, sorry) was a pain to get up but the descent offered one or two stunning viewpoints and was ample reward. Stopping for a photo at one I got chatting to an elderly Scottish couple. They kindly told me to stock up on bits in Lairg as there was nothing between there and Tongue! Thanking them for this advice, and after taking the opportunity to have a photo taken by them, I set off.

A quick feed stop in Bonar Bridge (steak slice and chocolate muffin, nutrition fans) and a chance to buy new batteries for the Garmin which was on the second pair of lithiums and finally running low. I couldn't help but curse the two days I'd accidentally left it on overnight...it would have survived the trip otherwise!

Bonar Bridge is about sixty miles from Loch Ness. The last half of the journey looked entertaining enough by the route profile alone. Little did I know quite how much more fun it was going to be...

Past Lairg and with just thirty five ('just thirty five'?! ha, listen to me now!) miles to go and the A836 changes from a 'normal' road. It becomes bleak. It becomes exposed. It becomes singletrack.

Oh yes. Not only was I now battling into a headwind with no shelter for miles, I also got to stop at random points to allow cars to pass.

Brilliant.

With my speed into the wind down to about nine miles an hour, it's fair to say I was a little demoralised. There wasn't any point cursing either, any sounds lost to to wind as soon as they were uttered.

At least there were the odd, cold, showers coming along at random points to cheer me up a bit...well, a monster headwind on its own would be too easy wouldn't it?!

It was a long thirty five miles and there really was nothing between Lairg and where I was heading.

It's so strange having travelled up from 'the bottom' to see just how sparse shops and services are up here, especially when compared to somewhere like the Lake District which has it's little village shops scattered upon the route.

I finally made it to Tongue (a really pretty approach to it, two miles of descent, with a lovely view over the sea) and found my way to the hostel, rolling in at just about half past eight. Nope, really...thirteen hours after setting off this morning. Like I said, a slog!

I ordered in a pizza on the recommendation of the hostel manager (it was that or shortbread, as nowhere's open in Tongue past half six!) and had a bit of a chat with the other residents before retiring for the night.

I got a feelin'...that tonight's gonna be a good night's sleep!

The winds had started to turn to the west as I settled in for the night. That would give me a lovely tail wind for the final leg should they stay.

What's the betting tomorrow is as calm and still a day you can imagine?! Sigh.

Stats for Tuesday 25th May 2010

Distance..113 miles
Time in saddle..9hrs 54mins
Average speed.....................................11.4mph
Maximum speed....................................29.2mph

Total distance to date..................................985 miles
Total time in saddle to date.................75hrs 18mins
Average speed for trip to date....................13.0mph

Wednesday 26th May 2010

Day Twelve: Tongue to John O'Groats

or, The One Where Now You're Gonna Believe Him...

Another good night's sleep and I was up early to get Day Eleven's blog finished and up before setting off on the final leg of the journey. I sat in the lounge with a cup of tea and two slices of home made cake (banana and chocolate) for my breakfast...well, with no shops around let alone open what else was I to do?!

All blogged up, fully packed and prepared I set out for what would hopefully be the final time at nine o'clock (does that count as early?). A lovely pootle along the water's edge, I was in high spirits and whistling along...

...until I hit the first hill. Which was in turn the first hill of a series of hills. Three quick peaks of 150, 250 and then 350 feet with drops back down to more or less sea level each time. The cycling equivalent of weightlifting supersets as it were!

Not going to lie...it was a struggle. Despite the favourable tailwind (yes, yes, oh yay...it had turned westerly!), my legs weren't obliging at all and it was a real effort to get myself up to the top each time. Perhaps that headwind the day before had taken it out of me...

A quick feed stop in Bettyhill at the first shop I'd seen open for miles and miles and then it was on to the last big climb of the trip. After labouring up the 500ft or so, I knew there were just five more climbs left of the journey, and not that many miles to go either!

With the wind finally offering a hand I made good time and stopped off for lunch at a Tesco in Thurso. With food inside me and less than thirty miles to go I knew as I set off that it was going to be my last stop of the trip.

The miles ticked over as the time passed and approaching Dunnet it was tempting to give a trip to Dunnet's Head a miss and just get to John O'Groats. I couldn't do that having taken in Lizard

on the way up though so I turned off into the wind and made my way up to the most northerly point.

Obligatory photo out of the way, I was back with the tail wind and after joining the main road once again the signs started appearing; 'John O'Groats 12', 'John O'Groats 9', 'John O'Groats 8'...it didn't matter by now, I knew I was going to finish!

Now, I'd heard that there's not a lot at John O'Groats and 'it's a little run down' but I didn't quite expect it to be as bad as it is. What. A. Dive!

I made my way down to the (now derelict) hotel and, as the clock ticked over to 16.05, crossed the finish line. Job done! The famous sign post is situated just a few yards up from the hotel and I wandered up to join the queue(!) of people wanting a picture taken. The pair in front of me were just embarking on their trip, picking up a momento to signal the start.

Photos at the post are now a commercial venture, with the sign coming down each night and unauthorised picture taking frowned upon...which is a bit sad really. Anyway, I paid my £9.95 to the surliest man I have ever met and got my picture taken. In the days of super fast broadband and instant communication it's quaint I'm going to have to wait seven to ten days for them to post it to me...sigh.

A hot chocolate over the road to celebrate (nope, no pub at the finish...that would be too much fun!), I had a chat with a couple of groups there. A family of bikers that were taking in Scotland and the Isles and a couple who had just completed a LEJOG as a solo rider and support vehicle. Earlier in the week I'd made the decision to change my plans of accommodation for the night and, rather than travel the twenty miles or so back to Scrabster to catch the ferry over to Stromness I booked into the John O'Groats youth hostel and onto a ferry from nearby Gills Bay the next day to

take me over to the Orkneys. With the wind as it was I was certainly glad to not be having to tackle that sort of distance back into it!

John O'Groats youth hostel has borrowed a lead from London Luton Airport, and is actually situated two and a half miles back along the coast from which you've already travelled! Having now finished, my legs had decided they wanted a rest and it was hard work convincing them they had to make this journey.

When I say there is nothing in John O'Groats it's no exaggeration. I went into the local shop to look for some food for the night but found nothing of interest at all and resigned myself to the fact I could just have the rest of the shortbread I had left with a cup of tea.

Whilst booking into the hostel I asked if there was anywhere to grab some food. After hearing that the closest place was two miles away I decided the shortbread would do!

I got to my room and was sorting through my stuff when there was a knock on the door. It was one of the bikers from the group I'd met earlier. They'd heard me ask about food and wanted to invite me to join them as they had plenty to go round. How nice!

A lovely pasta dish was the fare on offer with a glass of red wine on top, and chocolate and coffee to finish. It was nice to have a bit of a chat with the group and towards the end of the night another group checked in, ready for their John O'Groats to Lands End trip starting the next day. On a recumbent tandem that they built themselves! Chapeau!

They were in high spirits and with a big group together it really was a lovely end to what's been a trip with highs and lows but an excellent experience overall. A trip where me actually getting to and crossing the finish line was never in doubt. Not at all... (cough, cough)

I have been making a note of every penny I've spent and everything I've bought (mainly strawberry milk, Snickers and doughnuts to be fair!), so I'll update the blog once I'm back home.

I think I'll also get one more update in once I've finished on the Orkney Islands; just a few quick thoughts on the trip as a whole after having a couple of days to let it all sink in...so that's something for you to look forward to!

Finally, I'd just like to say thank you to everybody that has been in touch over the last twelve days. On the way back from the Essex Lambs Sportive I got chatting to two guys who said you go through some dark patches on a solo trip like this...they weren't wrong, but your comments and encouragement did help me carry on.

As did the sponsorship that anybody who has donated put forward. It's nice to know that me completing this challenge and getting sponsored along the way is going to help The Stroke Association with their work. If you were waiting to see if I actually finished before sponsoring me (I know there was a couple!) then, don't worry, the link is still active; http://www.justgiving.com/onemanandlejog

Thank you.

Stats for Wednesday 26th May 2010

Distance	71 miles
Time in saddle	5hrs 8mins
Average speed	13.8mph
Maximum speed	38.9mph
Total distance to date	1,056 miles
Total time in saddle to date	80hrs 26mins
Average speed for trip to date	13.1mph

ORKNEY ISLANDS

Orkney Islands and the Journey Home

After a evening of food and good company I was up reasonably early to see off the group that had arrived last night. As I mentioned last night, hats off to them and best of luck. If you want to keep up with their progress then take a look at their blog at: http://www.2men1bike.co.uk

With the closest shop about two miles away and the hostel offering no food at all I had to head out to get breakfast. I'd managed to negotiate a bit the night before and arranged to get breakfast from a friend of the hostel owner's over the road. So at nine o'clock I pottered over to see what was on offer...

A full fry up, a good natter about the state of John O'Groats and its future later and I knew it was a good idea.

Not having a distance to cover for the day felt a little weird and the rain falling from the grey sky did little to lift spirits! On leaving the hostel I had three hours to kill before the ferry was due to depart. Having done John O'Groats the day before I really didn't fancy heading back in the gloom...it was depressing enough in the sunlight! I opted instead for a pootle along the coast back towards Thurso.

I stopped off after a mile or so to take a look around Canisbay's church. It's a lovely, peaceful place and was the church that the Queen Mother regularly attended. It's also the home of the stone laid by John De Groat back in the 1600s.

After leaving the church I carried on to a small cafe, the Tea Cosy, which is also home to a craft shop displaying local artist's work. After looking round the pieces of art I settled down with a hot chocolate and cake and had a read of the local paper to kill off the rest of the time I had to wait (top local news story? A girl has bought a t-shirt printing machine and has produced shirts for a local 10k race).

I got to Gills Bay and boarded the ferry over to the Orkneys. The hour long journey was a little choppy in places, the uneasy sea due to the gods stirring salt into the sea at that point according to mythology (I thought that was quite cute). After landing at St. Margaret's Hope I cycled off towards Kirkwall...

The Orkneys are hillier than I imagined. Not steep but slow climbs, and ever so green - especially when compared to the brown nothingness I'd experienced in the Highlands the couple of days before.

I stopped off at the Italian Chapel en route, a place of worship built by Italian prisoners of war during the Second World War out of two Nissen huts; its interior is beautifully painted.

Over a couple of Churchill Barriers (built to stop German U-Boats) and I was nearly there. Three miles to go and 'crack'...my freehub went!

Basically the freehub is the bit that makes the back wheel turn as you pedal. Well, no matter how fast I pedalled it wasn't going anywhere. Sigh.

I covered the final three miles in a freewheel / push / pedal method (it occasionally engaged, just for laughs) and went into Orkney Cycles for a diagnosis. He confirmed my thoughts and advised I return to Geoffrey Butler as it should be under warranty. That'll be a fun trip on my return!

I finally made it to the hostel and opted for an early night after picking up some excellent fish and chips which were by far the best of the trip!

With the bike not co-operating quite as I'd like it to, I decided to book myself onto a coach trip for the next day so that I could see the sights that the island has to offer.

DONALD GROT SONE TO JHONE GROT
LAID ME HEIR APRLL XIIIDAY 1568 LCWYS
AND DONALALD GROT JONE GROT AND
HIS GONAIELD LAD AND THAAR
FAORBARS OF DONALD WHOUSE GOD
CALD ME YE XIIIDAY OF APRLL ANNO
DOMINY M.D.L. 1586

AMIORALE.

I'm glad I did as the weather swayed between sunshine and showers during the day (two hundred and forty days of rain a year in the Orkneys, weather fans!). It was good to see the sights with a running commentary and it gave me a chance to learn a bit about the history of the islands that I wouldn't have done had I been on my bike.

After seeing pretty much all the island has to offer, including the 3,500 B.C. settlement at Scara Brae and the Standing Stones, the tour was done and I had seven hours to fill before my ferry back to Aberdeen.

I wandered Kirkwall and stopped in a few bars for a while, before grabbing an excellent meal at The Shore and deciding it was worth getting a taxi over to the ferry terminal (well, it was raining!).

It was at the ferry terminal I bumped into a familiar face, someone I'd chatted to in the Loch Ness hostel a few days before. It was nice to have a bit of a chat and share the experience with someone else who had just done the End-to-End.

Although I had a sleeper seat booked the cinema was done for the night and was available so I settled in for the night. Drifting off on the recliner I got about an hour's sleep in before waking up with two dead legs. The seat wasn't working so I decided to try the floor…as had most of the others in the room!

Come five o'clock there was no chance of me getting any more sleep so I went for a wander around the ship. It was amusing to see the state of the place; like a war film or zombie flick bodies were spread everywhere, people grabbing any opportunity to get some shut-eye…a really glamorous way to travel!

We docked at 07.00 and I made my way over to Aberdeen station to wait for my 09.52 train back home. Settling into the coffee shop, I took advantage of the power socket available next to my table and killed time online before boarding.

The train trip was long and busy, students heading back for Easter from St. Andrews (Leuchars) filling the coaches with bags upon bags.

The sights you can see from the east coast mainline train are incredible north of the border with the trainline hugging the coast and it was nice to get a decent view out over the Forth Bridge having been over it on the bike in the fog the week before.

People do say it's hard to get back from John O'Groats, and I'd be inclined to agree. It took me (not including waiting times between them) an hour long ferry over to the Orkneys, a seven hour ferry journey back to Aberdeen, a seven hour train journey to London Kings Cross and a half hour cycle back to Shepherds Bush but…I was home!

One final lot of updates to go before this blog is finished for all intents and purposes (try to hold back the tears…). I've got the food list to put up once it's all compiled, the cost of the trip to tot up and publish and a 'final thoughts' bit where I'm going to try and sum it all up into a few paragraphs…stay tuned!

Stats for the Orkney Islands

It doesn't matter any more…woo hoo!

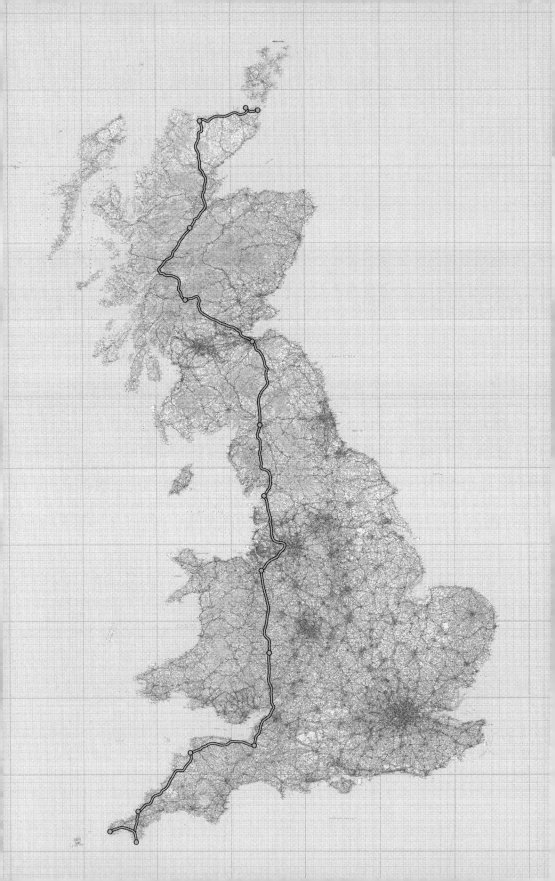

Epilogue: Final Thoughts

So then, my final thoughts on the trip? I don't think that a LEJOG is a hard journey per se; it is, after all, simply a case of getting on your bike and pedalling yourself from A to B daily! My training certainly wasn't anywhere near the sort of distance or volume that is recommended as necessary to undertake this challenge; I only completed two rides of over one hundred miles before setting off!

That's not to say I didn't enjoy doing it, though. I've seen an extremely thin slice of this country in a way that very few people can say they have and there's moments I recall fondly now and hopefully will do for many more months and years to come.

Having never blogged before, I'm really glad that I decided to start doing so for this journey. I'd hazard a guess that I spent two to three hours a night doing so, but people that were following have told me that they appreciated it and it has also given me something special to look back on, and provided me with the content to produce this book!

I'm pleased with all of my kit decisions bar the Carradice! I never once felt like I didn't have enough, or that I'd carried too much with me. My Garmin HCx may well have taken a bit of 'magic' out of the navigation of each day, but certainly made the whole process less stressful. I'd perhaps go as far to recommend one to anybody attempting a similar journey ahead of anything else.

I was surprised to see how much I spent over the twelve days although, to be fair, around a third of the total money that went through my hands was on bike repairs that nobody could have honestly foreseen. Certainly not the rack for my bag failing on Day Two! Otherwise I think that I got reasonable value for money for everything else considering.

Splitting my overnight stops between B&Bs, hotels and hostels may well have added extra cost to my journey, but I think it was worth it overall. Perhaps if I had a support vehicle or others with me then camping would have added to the adventure but I think the way I approached it was best for a solo attempt.

On that note, I have been asked by many people why I chose to do my LEJOG solo and unsupported, and also if I was lonely on the way?

First of all I decided to undertake the trip on my own as, whilst I was confident I could complete the distance, I wasn't sure of my own abilities on the bike and didn't want to be the one slowing a group down. Having now completed it, and read other encounters I don't think I would have done but I don't regret doing it alone at all. It's a hell of a party story if nothing else!

I can honestly say that the only time I felt alone was as I realised I was the only sober individual amongst a bustling Princes Street in Edinburgh on Day Eight. As I wandered along that street all I wanted to be was back home. On reflection, a Saturday night stopover in a big city after the previous few days probably wasn't the best choice!

In conclusion, did I enjoy the trip? Yes, without a doubt. It's made me appreciate the island on which we live in ways I certainly didn't before. It's certainly opened my eyes as to how beautiful parts of it can be, and I'm sure I'm not the only one who's gone end-to-end that looks on as the map scrolls behind the television weatherman without thinking 'bloody hell...I've cycled that!'.

Would I do it again? No, probably not. Certainly not in that direction anyway, and probably not solo if I was to go from top to bottom. That trip's been done, it's onto the next challenge now I'm afraid.

What's next? You'll just have to wait and see...

Appendix I: The Kit

Having now completed my LEJOG, I thought it would probably make sense to let people know what it was I took with me on my trip. As my journey from one end of the country to the other was going to be solo and without any support vehicle at all, it was a case of packing as little and as light as possible.

With enough of me to carry around anyway I didn't really fancy lugging any extra kilograms uphill so, for that reason, I committed myself to a small saddlebag and decided that if it didn't fit in there or in my jersey pockets it wasn't going with me!

In short, I travelled light. Very light. I had two lots of cycling gear which I alternated daily, some extra bits and pieces for if the weather turns during the day and also a set of clothes for the evenings. So, here's what's went with me…

The Bike
Bianchi Via Nirone 7 Alu C2C 105. I've called her Daphne.

The Bag
Initially it was a Carradice Barley saddlebag with an SQR system to attach it to the bike. After that failed on Day Two I moved onto a Giant bag and generic lightweight rack that attached to the seatpost.

The Cycling Kit
2 x Uni-Qlo Smooth Dry V-neck t-shirt base-layers
2 x Santini Genesis One Bibshorts
2 x Shutt Sportive LE Jerseys
2 x pairs of DeFeet Woolie Boolie Socks
1 x pair of Specialized BG Sport Mitts
1 x pair of Specialized BG Sport Road Shoes
…and, of course, a cycle helmet! A Giro Monza.

Extra Cycle Clothing
1 x Gore Bike Wear Path (Rain)Jacket
1 x pair of Prendas Meraklon Arm Warmers
1 x pair of Santini Sirio Super Roubaix Leg Warmers
1 x pair of DeFeet Dura Gloves
1 x Merino Wool Buff
1 x pair of Bolle Contour Safety Glasses

Eveningwear
1 x Uni-Qlo Heat Tech V-Neck Long-Sleeved T-Shirt
1 x Uni-Qlo lightweight 3/4 length trousers
1 x pair of Uni-Qlo Smooth Dry Boxer Shorts
1 x pair of flip-flops

Toiletries
1 x travel-sized toothbrush and toothpaste
1 x travel-sized shower gel
1 x travel-sized deodorant
1 x 100ml tub of P20 Once-a-Day Sunscreen
1 x tub of Assos Chamois Cream

Gadgets and Technology
1 x Apple iPhone (used to update blog on the way)
1 x Apple iPhone Charger
1 x Roberts Sports 995 Pocket Radio w/headphones
1 x Pentax Optio W60 Camera (and spare battery)
1 x Garmin eTrex Vista HCx (GPS / Sat-Nav)
4 x AA Lithium batteries (spares for Garmin)
2 x AAA batteries (spares for radio)

Spares and Repairs
2 x Specialized Inner Tubes
1 x Park Po2C Glueless Patch Kit
1 x Bontranger Air Support Mini Pump
1 x stretch of Duct Tape (wrapped around pump)
1 x Lezyne SV10 Multi-Tool
1 x pair of Surgical Scissors
Spare Power-Links (for chain repairs)
Cable Ties

Miscellaneous
2 x packs of Ibuprofen Tablets
1 x pack of Hydrocolloid Plasters
1 x Camelbak Podium Bottle
1 x Camelbak Podium Chill Bottle
1 x Coiled Bike Lock (for cafe stops)
1 x RoadID Ankle Bracelet
1 x set of Laminated Route Cards
1 x Mesh Bag (to help dry bits en route if necessary)
1 x Muji 'Pouch' (to keep bits in one place!)
Small Amount of Cash and Debit Card
Train Tickets (journey out to start and back home)

Appendix II: The Cost

There are a fair number of blogs and accounts of LEJOG journeys available on the Internet; a miscellany of maps, meanders and mishaps, yet not one offered even a rough idea as to how much the journey cost the traveller(s). It's for this reason that I decided before heading off to make a note of every penny I spent whilst on the road and I hope that the fact that I have done so does offer anybody planning a similar sort of trip a bit of insight as to the sort of costs they can expect.

I secured myself the cheapest train tickets possible for the journeys I wanted to make; the Aberdeen to London Kings Cross train being an absolute steal. I could have travelled during the day down to Lands End reducing that cost, but thought a sleeper service would offer me a decent night's sleep. In hindsight that was a mistake!

Obviously, undertaking this trip as a solo journey does make it a little more expensive - not having a support vehicle means you'll be carrying your own bits and pieces so there's no chance to buy in bulk. I'm pretty sure this is why the amount of money I spent on food and drink is as high as it is. I ended up spending c.£16.50 per day and I'm confident this could have been at least halved had I had a support vehicle which could have been loaded with meals and distributed them as and when they were necessary, also lightening my load.

Added on top of that is the fact that occupancy rates in any establishment are weighted in favour of those that aren't travelling alone (understandably) and it's not long until you see the costs start to creep, although I think the average of c.£22.50 per night isn't bad considering I had a roof to sleep under each night as opposed to a tent! Half of my accommodation costs also included breakfast the next morning which was a good way to start to the day.

I was unlucky with the repairs needed en route, but otherwise feel I did alright. in terms of how much I spent over the two weeks. I haven't included costs incurred whilst in the Orkney Islands as this was more of a 'holiday within a holiday' for me and not really part of my LEJOG.

Travel

London to Penzance (Sleeper Train)	£74.00
Gills Bay to St Margarets Hope (Ferry)	£13.00
Kirkwall Town to Kirkwall Port (Taxi)	£5.00
Kirkwall to Aberdeen (Ferry)	£21.70
Aberdeen to London (Train)	£15.00
Total Travel	*£128.70*

Accommodation

Penkerris B&B (St. Agnes)	£27.50
Westward Ho! YHA (Westward Ho!)	£15.50
Admiral Blake Guest House (Bridgwater)	£25.00
Holly Tree Guest House (Hereford)	£27.50
Chester Backpackers (Chester)	£25.00
The Westleigh Hotel (Morecambe)	£28.00
Arkale Lodge (Carlisle)	£25.00
Caledonian Backpackers (Edinburgh)	£21.00
Crianlarich SYHA (Crianlarich)	£20.50
Loch Ness SYHA (Loch Ness)	£19.00
Tongue SYHA (Tongue)	£18.50
John O'Groats SYHA (John O'Groats)	£19.00
Total Accommodation	*£271.50*

Food and Drink

Food and Drink	£200.09
Total Food and Drink	*£200.09*

Miscellaneous

Bike Repairs	£374.95
Medical Supplies	£4.65
Postage Costs to send Carradice(s) home	£5.24
Finish Photo	£9.95
Change Sacrificed (nightly)	£1.32
Total Miscellaneous	*£396.11*

TOTAL COST.. £996.40

Appendix III: The Food

FOOD CONSUMED OVER THE TWELVE DAYS
In numerical and then alphabetical order

29 x Brownies / Buns / Cakes / Muffins
(Made up of;   4 Cakes, 1 Chelsea Bun, 4 Currant Buns,
1 Chocolate Brownie, 1 Chocolate
Muffin, 5 Flapjacks, 1 Havva Cake, 5 Jaffa
Cake Bars, 6 Shortbread packets and
1 Sponge Cake)
28 x Snickers
10 x Packets of Sweets or Gum
(Made up of;   3 packs of Chewing Gum, 2 packs of
Foamy Bananas, 2 packs of Haribo,
2 KitKat Chunky and 1 pack of Maltesers)
9 x Doughnuts
8 x Rolls or Sandwiches
(Made up of;   1 BLT, 1 Brunch Triple, 1 Chicken and Mayo,
2 Chicken and Stuffing, 1 Chicken and
Sweetcorn, 1 Ham and Salad and 1 Tuna)
3 x Ice Creams
(Made up of;   2 Magnums and 1 Snickers)
3 x Pizzas
3 x Soreen
(Made up of;   2 loaves and 1 Snack Pack)
2 x Apple Pie and Custard
2 x Full English Fry-Ups
2 x Mule Bars
2 x Packets of Crisps
2 x Steak Slices
1 x Cheeseburger and Chips
1 x Chicken Pasta
1 x Chips
1 x Cod and Chips
1 x Steak & Kidney Pie, Chips and Peas
1 x Venison Burger and Chips
plus, one pack of frozen vegetables for the knee!

DRINK

27 x bottles of Coca-Cola
26 x bottles of Milkshake
3 x bottles of Lucozade Sport
3 x bottles of Orange Juice
1 x bottle of Oasis Orange
plus, the obligatory one cup of tea!

In a similar vein to Appendix II: The Cost, I was also keen to see quite how much food and drink that I got through during the twelve days.

At the same time as noting down how much everything was costing I also made sure I kept a record of what it was I was purchasing and, if relevant, consuming.

Whilst I fully appreciate it's not the healthiest of diets, it got me from one end of the country without any incidents in terms of food intake or lack of it. It is perhaps unsurprising, however, after seeing this list to hear that I only lost around 1kg (2.2lbs) during the twelve days, despite pedalling my way over one thousand miles - it's certainly not a diet of a professional athlete!

It should also be noted that this record is only taken from the moment I crossed the start line on Saturday 15th May 2010 up to and including the moment I crossed the finish line on Wednesday 26th May 2010.

Acknowledgements

Thanks to:

Paul and Neil at Planet Bike, Barnstaple, for getting me back on track on Day Three; replacing my broken Carradice rack with a new solution. Without you guys I'm not sure I'd have made Bristol, let alone John O'Groats!

Mark at Coombes Cycles, Hereford for lubing me up on Day Five (ooo-er!). Whilst it didn't solve the real problem it didn't half make the morning's cycling far more pleasant.

Dorothy (and her dog Max!) in Chester. Inviting me in for a cup of tea and the use of your tumbledryer was unexpected but ever so welcome. I hope I didn't bore you too much!

Ellis at The Edge Cycleworks, Chester. You may have cost me the most money on my trip, but if it wasn't for your diagnosis of a 'dodgy' crank I'm not sure Daphne would have made it all the way to the top - you've also set me up with a fully 105-equipped bike, so can't really complain I guess!

Pat at Arkale Lodge, Carlisle. I will happily admit to feeling a little choked up as I went to bed on Day Seven. You had no need to do what you did, but your hospitality restored my faith in people. You are a true gentleman.

Jo at Nevis Cycles, Fort William for fixing the broken spoke on Day Eleven. My last trip to a bike shop en route to the top but just as important as the first!

All of the readers of my blog. Knowing that people were reading up on me and my progress was a big motivation to keep those pedals turning. Whilst I enjoyed getting it done every day it was the first time I've ever written to an audience, so apologies if it wasn't quite up to scratch!

Thank you.

2847057R00043

Printed in Great Britain
by Amazon.co.uk, Ltd.,
Marston Gate.